A NEW LIFE IN CANADA

The Letters of Sophia Eastwood,

1843 - 1870

SUSAN BEATTIE

CANADIAN SCHOLARS' PRESS INC.   TORONTO   1989

A New Life in Canada

First published in 1989 by
Canadian Scholars' Press Inc.
211 Grenadier Road
Toronto, M6R 1R9
Canada.

Canadian Cataloguing in Publication Data:

Eastwood, Sophia
A new life in Canada

ISBN 0-921627-40-8

1. Eastwood, Sophia - Correspondence. 2. Frontier and pioneer life - Canada.
3. Pioneers - Canada - Correspondence. I. Beattie, Susan, 1934- .
II. Title.

FC471.E28A4 1988   971.04   C89-093092-9
F1032.E28A4 1988   7503/

Table of Contents

	Page
Acknowledgements	3
To the Teacher	5
A Family Tree	6
Introduction	7
The Eastwood Family in Canada and England	13

The Letters:

Part One: The Journey	15
Part Two: Into the Wildwood	31
Part Three: At Home in Upper Canada	52

Activities and Exercises:

Part One	67
Part Two	71
Part Three	74
Extensions	78
Independent Learning	78

Glossary	79
Metric Conversions	83
Photo Credits	84

Acknowledgements

This book would not have been possible without the work of Audrey Chacksfield of Sussex, England, the owner of these letters. She made a typescript copy of the originals which she thoughtfully deposited in the Baldwin Room of the Toronto Metro-Central Library. I wish to thank her for making the letters available and for granting me permission to publish them in this form. *A New Life In Canada* developed out of work begun for a project sponsored by the Modern Languages Department at the Ontario Institute for Studies in Education. I would like to thank Joan Howard, coordinator of the project, for her help during its early stages. I am grateful to the staff of the Baldwin Room, Metro-Central Library, Toronto, for their assistance and to Shelagh Ross and Jack Wayne of Canadian Scholars' Press Inc. for the care they have taken in the production of this book. I would like particularly to thank my husband, John, for his advice and encouragement.

To the Teacher

The principal aim of *A New Life In Canada* is to provide students and teachers with authentic and original Canadian material.

The letters of Sophia Eastwood, an unknown pioneer woman, are published here for the first time. They tell in her words the story of individuals in a maturing family, of their lives as pioneers in the Canadian woods, and of the growing community in which they lived. The letters show the importance of each to the others.

A New Life In Canada has been developed with the Ontario Schools Intermediate and Senior (O.S.I.S.) Guidelines for English and History in mind. It is designed for use in English, History, and Canadian Studies courses. It is also suitable for use with students of English as a Second Language who have reached an intermediate or higher level. They will find in these letters many experiences parallel to their own.

The authenticity of the content and the clear, direct voice of Sophia Eastwood make *A New Life In Canada* appropriate for use at all levels of study through intermediate and senior high school and among college and adult groups. The family context and the intensity of the experience the letters describe provide a natural opportunity to stimulate the historical and literary imaginations of the students who read them.

A wide variety of optional activities accompany the text. These have been grouped at the back of the book in three parts reflecting the arrangement of the letters. They include suggestions for writing, speaking, and responding in a variety of modes and registers and for different purposes. There are, in addition, opportunities for the exploration and use of drama, art, graphics, and other forms of media. Many of the tasks have been planned for groups and pairs. The activities are followed by suggestions for extended and independent learning.

A NEW LIFE IN CANADA

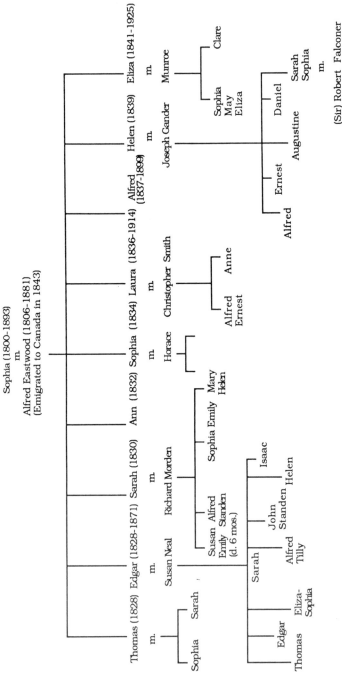

Sophia (1800-1893)
m.
Alfred Eastwood (1806-1881)
(Emigrated to Canada in 1843)

Thomas (1828) Edgar (1828-1871) Sarah (1830) Ann (1832) Sophia (1834) Laura (1836-1914) Alfred (1837-1899) Helen (1839) Eliza (1841-1925)

m.   m.   m.   m.   m.   m.
                Susan Neal   Richard Morden   Horace   Christopher Smith   Joseph Gander   Munroe

Sophia   Sarah

Susan Alfred   Sophia Emily   Mary
Emily Standen   Helen
(d. 6 mos.)

Alfred Ernest   Alfred Ernest   Clare
Ernest   Sophia
Sarah   May
Isaac   Eliza

John   Anne
Standen Helen

Alfred
Tilly

Edgar   Eliza-
Thomas Sophia

Alfred   Ernest   Daniel

Augustine   Sarah
            Sophia

m.

(Sir) Robert Falconer

6

Introduction

Sophia and Alfred Eastwood emigrated to British North America from Sussex, England in 1843. They brought with them seven of their nine children, leaving two, Thomas and Laura, with Sophia's parents on their farm in England. Over the next twenty-seven years Sophia wrote letters first to her parents and later to her daughter Laura who remained in Sussex. It is these letters that provide the contents of this volume.

Sophia's letters are of special interest because they tell from the point of view of an ordinary woman the experience of a pioneer family in Canada. The pioneer setting enhances the story of the Eastwood family as it unfolds, but the central figure throughout is Sophia, the mother of nine children who, at the age of forty-four, undertook to raise them in the "heart of the forest". Through her portrayal of the family's efforts to establish a new life in Upper Canada, Sophia Eastwood gives focus and shape to the larger pioneer experience.

The letters of this unknown woman parallel in an interesting way the work of other pioneer women writers. The most well known of these is her exact contemporary, Susanna Moodie, whose autobiographical account of pioneer life, *Roughing It In The Bush*, is a Canadian classic. The two women's lives followed a similar course. They were born within three years of each other, Sophia Eastwood in 1800, Susanna Moodie in 1803. Both emigrated from England to Upper Canada where they settled in the woods. But while the Moodies eventually abandoned their attempts to establish a farm in the bush, the Eastwoods, who were already seasoned farmers when they left England, persevered. Sophia's letters chronicle her family's essentially successful experience. Her natural language, direct and unembellished, adds texture and immediacy to the story she tells, a story that provides a valuable and interesting supplement to *Roughing It In The Bush* and an addition to existing pioneer literature.

The collection contains twenty-six letters, twenty-three of which were written by Sophia. Twenty-two letters are included in this volume. They are published here for the first time with permission of Laura's descendant in Sussex where the originals may be found. The letters reproduced here are in typescript copy in the Metropolitan Central Library, Toronto. Although spelling and punctuation have been modernized and some repetition omitted, the content and language are unchanged except where necessary to clarify meaning.

The letters fall naturally into three parts, each reflecting a stage in the Eastwoods' new lives. The first group of letters begins the correspondence in 1843 with Sophia's description of the departure from England, the ocean voyage, and the safe arrival at Quebec. These letters tell of the problems confronting the family during their first year and a half in Upper Canada concluding with their move into the forest. Part Two contains letters written between 1845 and 1851. They provide a description of the family during the pioneer stage of their lives. The final group of letters describes the second house, mentioned as a dream so many years before, the productive farm, and the lives of the children, some of whom were now parents themselves.

＊　　＊　　＊　　＊　　＊　　＊　　＊　　＊　　＊

The Eastwoods' journey from England to British North America began at the London Docks on Saturday April 20, 1843. There they boarded the sailing vessel for a voyage that was to last for thirty-five days. They sailed down the River Thames, reaching Gravesend on April 21. It was here that Sophia wrote and posted her first letter. From Gravesend their ship sailed out of the Thames, through the Straits of Dover, and into the English Channel. On April 23 they arrived at Portsmouth where they prepared for the long voyage across the Atlantic Ocean, and on April 26 they sailed for Quebec arriving just a month later.

In her first four letters Sophia told the story of this journey and of its continuation up the St. Lawrence into Upper Canada. In them she described the sights from the water and the conditions on board the ship. The Eastwoods had begun their voyage in middle steerage, a crowded and uncomfortable area between decks. They arranged to move to more spacious quarters, however, and it was with a tone of relief that Sophia mentioned in her letter from Quebec how well all the children were at the end of the crossing. Many in middle steerage had been ill, and two children had died and been committed, as she reported, to the "mighty deep" (Letter #3). The ocean crossing did indeed prove to be uneventful for everyone in the family except Sophia herself. She suffered from violent seasickness, so much so that she vowed never to "go aboard a ship again" (#3).

The Eastwoods' journey was not to end with their safe arrival at Quebec. From there they continued by steamer to Montreal where they hoped to settle and begin farming. Sophia and the children waited there a week while Alfred walked a hundred miles into the countryside to try to find acquaintances from Sussex and a suitable place for the family to live. He found that the land was "cold and stoney and could not grow any wheat," and so they moved on further west toward Upper Canada (#4). After travelling for three days and nights they reached Kingston. There they followed the advice of an "English gentleman" and made their way to Picton and then to Bloomfield, a nearby village, where they were offered temporary accommodation. Two of the children, Edgar and Sarah, immediately found work as servants with local families (#4).

The Eastwoods spent their first year in Upper Canada in Bloomfield. The months that followed their arrival were difficult ones. They had few possessions and became increasingly concerned about establishing a new life in Canada without land of their own. Unfortunately, they had used almost all their money travelling and they had little prospect of earning enough to buy a farm. On November 28, 1843, Alfred wrote to Sophia's parents. In this, his only letter, he explained the family's circumstances and asked Sophia's father for a loan of forty sovereigns (pounds) which he said would enable him to "get a farm of fifty acres and bring my family up and do well here." Meanwhile he hired himself out to a farmer to make sure of having work through the first difficult winter (#5).

Fortunately, Sophia's parents were able to send the money Alfred asked for. When Sophia next wrote, on June 29, 1844, a year after their arrival, the family had moved to Rawdon, later to become Stirling, fourteen miles north of Belleville in Hastings County. There they had taken a hundred acres of "wild land" with the intention of moving "right into the heart of the forest." The move into the woods meant years of hard physical work, but it had much to recommend it too. Not least, the Eastwoods would own their own farm on land Sophia described to her parents as "first rate" (#6).

Sophia and Alfred took five of their children with them when they moved to Rawdon. They left Sarah and a younger sister, Sophia, in Bloomfield where they were hired out to the families they had met a year earlier. The girls received a little money along with their room and board. Sarah was by then fourteen; Sophia, just ten. It was a consolation to their mother to know they would be sent to school through the winter. Edgar, the oldest son, now sixteen, accompanied his parents. Ann, the second daughter, also went with her parents. Although she was twelve and old enough to hire out, she suffered from poor health and was unable to work. Seven-year-old Alfred was a continuing source of concern to Sophia, for while he grew nicely, he did not "improve much in his talk" (#6). The two youngest children, Helen and Eliza, were five and three when the family moved into the bush, and Sophia herself was forty-four.

    *   *   *   *   *   *   *   *   *

The second group of letters follows the Eastwoods through the most strenuous years of their lives. In 1844 they settled in the forest and began to make it home. Their neighbours helped them get started in the bush by building their first house, a shanty, but it was on their own efforts and abilities that they eventually had to depend. Edgar worked alongside his father. Together they cut a road into the land and began the massive task of transforming the forest into fields by chopping, burning, and plowing. By March, 1845, their first spring in the bush, they had about sixteen acres cleared and ready to plant. They gradually cleared and cultivated their land, and they increased their stock to include cattle, pigs, and sheep. Their first source of income had been potash, which they made from ashes, but by the fall of 1846 they had grown enough wheat to have a supply for themselves and some to sell (#10).

The apparently steady progress they made in improving their circumstances was not without obstacles and set-backs. Sophia's life during this period was far from easy. She had her share of fever and ague along with the notably hard work of a pioneer woman (#12). She had particular concerns too about the growth and development of her children. Young Alfred continued to develop slowly, and Ann's health improved only slightly. Edgar suffered a serious injury when he cut his foot with an axe and could not work for several months (#11). Nor was the family in England far from her mind. Sophia still expected to be reunited with Laura, and she continued to express the hope in her letters that someone trustworthy could be found to bring Laura to them in Canada (#15).

Sophia and Alfred found much that was new to them in Upper Canada and in spite of the intense work and lack of money, they expressed satisfaction with the course their lives were taking. Sophia remarked frequently on the differences between the old life and their new one. She found it a great relief to be freed from tithes and taxes, and she noted that pigs and cattle could forage without restraint in the nearby woods. She commented on such new and diverse experiences as making soap, growing musk melons, and riding in a sleigh over ice. But apart from her children, the subject that most absorbed her was the farm, and the need to turn a substantial area of the forest into productive farmland if they were to survive and raise their family successfully in the Canadian woods.

In 1847 Thomas Mann, recently arrived from Sussex and an agent for the Agricultural Society, called on the Eastwoods at the request of Sophia's father. His letter, included in Part Two, provides an interesting comment on the family's health, farm, and neighbourhood from the point of view of an outsider. He found them to be "tolerable comfortable and getting pretty well seasoned to the bush" (#12).

The period between 1844 and 1851 saw changes in the family as well as in the farm. Sarah and Edgar both married. Sarah, who had stayed barely a week with her family since their arrival in Canada, married Richard Morden, whom Sophia described as "a sober and industrious young man, bred and born in Bloomfield." Soon after they were married they moved with Richard's father to a "newly settled part of Upper Canada" about 250 miles away (#14). Edgar married Susan Neal, a young woman originally from Norfolk, England. They remained in Rawdon where Edgar had a share of his father's farm. Their first child was born in 1849. The Eastwoods' second youngest daughter, Helen, just ten at the time of Sarah's marriage, went to Bloomfield in the fall of 1849 to take Sarah's place with the family there. In England, Thomas also married, and his first child, a daughter named Sophia, was born in 1846.

Meanwhile, Rawdon continued to grow and develop. In 1849 Sophia wrote that a school had been built about a mile from their farm. This was a

INTRODUCTION

welcome addition to the community that by now had two mills and four stores. For Sophia, it meant that all the children would soon be able to go to school (#13). By the middle of the century, eight years after their arrival in Canada, Sophia and Alfred Eastwood had survived their most strenuous years, in spite of illness and serious injury. Although their lives were never to be easy, their most difficult years were behind them.

*   *   *   *   *   *   *   *   *

The third part of the Eastwoods' story begins in 1857 after a gap of five years in the correspondence. The family had been in Upper Canada for fourteen years. By then the farm was well established and productive, and the children were almost grown. Eliza, the youngest, was now sixteen. Sophia's letters reveal that these years were far from serene, however. Family members on both sides of the Atlantic experienced unexpected and occasionally tragic losses. Sarah and Richard lost their baby son at the age of six months. Later Richard himself died, and Sarah was left with three children and little means of support. Edgar was not to find life easy either. His health had always been delicate and he was often unable to work because of illness or accident. He suffered his most debilitating injury, however, when his horse shied and threw him. He broke his collarbone and could not use his hand or arm or work at farming for many months (#19).

Clearly the children had gained from their parents' resilience and the ability to persevere, for in spite of their losses and difficulties, they managed to continue their lives with reasonable success. Sarah rented out her farm. She then used what money she had to establish herself as a milliner and dressmaker in Walkerton. Edgar developed his interest in butchering and buying and selling livestock. This proved a useful line of work. It was less demanding physically than farming, and with the community growing there was a good market for meat. Even so, Edgar did not outlive his parents. He died in 1871, a year after Sophia's last letter.

By 1870 when the correspondence ends, all the children except Alfred had left the farm to live independently. Helen married the local minister's son and Eliza married a neighbouring blacksmith. Ann's health eventually improved enough for her to start her own business. The Eastwoods' son Alfred stayed on the farm with his parents. He remained "slow in his understanding" but he was a great help to them with the farm work in their later years (#20).

The Eastwoods' family, their farm, the community in which they lived, and Upper Canada itself, developed and matured together. Sophia made little mention of the world outside her experience, but she occasionally noted in passing, events of general interest or significance. She mentioned the construction of the Grand Trunk Railroad (#16) and the nearby iron ore mining town (#21.) for example, and such larger events as the War Between the States (#19) and the

11

Fenian Raids (#20). But for Sophia the most significant development of these years was the arrival of photography. She was at last able to see her daughter Laura and her grandchildren in England. At the end of her letters as at the beginning it was Sophia's family that mattered most to her.

With the passage of time Sophia wrote less frequently. Her last letter was written in 1870 when she was seventy years old. She was to live on the farm in Rawdon for another twenty-three years and die there in her ninety-fourth year. Her letters are a rich source of information about family life and work in nineteenth century Canada. But the real strength of the letters is in the voice of Sophia Eastwood herself as she worked to make a home for her family in the Canadian woods. Her letters to England record in direct and vivid language the experience of an ordinary family in rural Ontario during its pioneer stages. To discover her feelings, it is perhaps best to turn to her own words. "If you were here I should never want to go to England," wrote Sophia in her last letter to Laura. Canada had become her home.

The Eastwood Family

The Family in Canada

Sophia: Writer of most of the letters in *A New Life In Canada*. She was born in Sussex, England and emigrated to Upper Canada in 1843. Sophia, her husband Alfred, and five of their nine children settled in the Canadian woods in 1844. She died in 1893.

Alfred: Sophia's husband. He was born in England in 1806. As an experienced farmer he was able to use his knowledge of farming to choose good land and do well in Canada. Alfred died in 1881.

Edgar: Son of Sophia and Alfred. He emigrated to Upper Canada with the family at the age of fifteen. He had several occupations including farming and butchering. Edgar married Susan Neal and they had eight children. He died in 1871.

Sarah: The Eastwoods' oldest daughter. She was thirteen at the time of emigration. Sarah lived as a servant with a family in Bloomfield. She married Richard Morden and had four children, one of whom died in infancy. She was later widowed and went into business as a dressmaker.

Ann: The second daughter. She suffered from rheumatics as a child and was not able to work outside the family. As an adult she established a successful business. She did not marry.

Sophia: Nine years old when the family emigrated. Sophia was hired out to live with a Quaker family in Bloomfield soon after the Eastwoods arrived in Upper Canada. She married and had [two] daughters.

Alfred: The third and youngest son. He was six years old at the time of emigration. Alfred was a source of concern to Sophia as a child because he was slow in his understanding. As an adult he remained at home on the farm where he helped his parents. He died six years after his mother in 1899.

Helen: Four years old in 1843. She was hired out in Sarah's place in 1849. Helen married Joseph Gander who lived on the farm next to the Eastwoods. He became a Presbyterian minister. They had five children, one of whom marrried Sir Robert A. Falconer who became president of the University of Toronto.

Eliza: Youngest of the nine children. She was two years old when the family left England. She married a local blacksmith and they had two children. Eliza died in 1925.

The Family in England

The Standens: Sophia's parents in Sussex, England. They were hop farmers and owned their own farm, Miskins, which they later sold. It was to them that Sophia wrote many of her letters. Sophia never returned to England, but her father visited her in Canada.

Thomas: The oldest son. He remained with his grandparents in England when the family emigrated. He married and had two children. Thomas had mixed success as a farmer in England and eventually emigrated to North America. His first wife died, but he later remarried. Sophia addressed him frequently in her early letters.

Laura: One of the Eastwoods' six daughters. She was seven years old when the family emigrated. She was too ill to travel with them and remained with her grandparents in Sussex where she eventually married. Much of the later correspondence was to her, and it was she who saved the letters. Laura died in 1914.

PART ONE: THE JOURNEY

Letter 1

Gravesend
April 21st, 1843

Dear Father and Mother,

We thought you would be glad to hear that we are safe arrived at Gravesend. We started from London Dock yesterday afternoon and passed the first bridge just as the o'clock struck five, and we sailed into the basin and lay there all night. We started at five o'clock this morning with a steamer tugged to the vessel for Gravesend where we are just arrived at a quarter past ten o'clock.

The children are all quite well and highly delighted with their ride down the river [Thames]. It was such a fine morning. It was beautiful to see the country and things on the water. Little Alfred seems very happy. I wish you could all see us on board.

It is a large fine ship. I cannot tell you how many there are on board but nearly 200 and a great many more coming. There are from eighty to ninety in a small part where we are and a great many more expected. The ship is so large that we cannot feel it move at all on the river. We had gone many miles yesterday before I knew we were started.

Alfred's cold was very bad for the first day or two but he is much better now. The girls and Edgar all send their best love to their grandfather and grandmother and to Thomas and little Laura. We will write to you again when we get to Portsmouth. Please give our kindest love to Thomas and dear little Laura, and please accept the same yourselves from your ever affectionate son and daughter,

Alfred and Sophia Eastwood

Letter 2

Portsmouth
April 23, 1843

Dear Father and Mother,

When we wrote to you before we were lying at Gravesend. We sailed from there on Saturday afternoon into the basin and lay at anchor all night. In the morning the wind was fair and we sailed all day and came in sight of many beautiful places. We saw the Isle of Sheppey and lay at anchor in sight of Deal all night. The wind turned so that we could not sail on. On Monday morning we started again and we passed Dover Point and came in view of Dover Castle and the Cliffs. We were three miles from it [Dover Castle]. It was the prettiest sight we ever saw. We could see the coast of France, and we saw Hastings and the other places we passed in the night. This morning, Tuesday, the first thing we went on deck to see was the Isle of Wight. It appeared to be a very pretty place. We saw that about six o'clock this morning, and about two hours after we arrived safe at Portsmouth. We are going to stop here until Friday.

I am happy to say that we are all in good health and hope and trust you are the same. We have no seasickness worth speaking of yet. The children are all hearty and well and seem to enjoy themselves very much. We are moved in another part of the ship since we wrote to you where it is not so full, and we are

PART ONE: THE JOURNEY

as comfortable as if were in a house, but the middle steerage is very full and a great many of them are sick.

Our provisions keep very good yet. We have got a plum pudding for dinner today. The flour and raisins we had given to us in the ship.

I suppose I shall not be able to write any more until we land which, should it please the Lord to send such weather as we have had, will not be very long. Please give our kindest love to Thomas and dear little Laura. We hope she is happy. Sophia says I am to tell her how she likes riding on the sea. Edgar and the little girls all send their kindest love to their grandfather and grandmother and please accept the same from your

affectionate son and daughter

A NEW LIFE IN CANADA

Letter 3

Quebec
May 26th, 1843

My dear Father and Mother,

We have the pleasure of telling you we arrived safely at Quebec about the middle of last night. Thank the Lord we have had a comfortable voyage and much quicker than we could expect. The children are all healthy and well and have not been seasick, not worth speaking of. Edgar and his father were a little sick one morning and that was all, but I was very sick for three weeks and could not do anything for myself. I think nothing will ever induce me to go aboard a ship again, please God I get safe on land.

We have not had so much as a gale of wind to alarm us, and our captain and all the crew are extremely kind and civil. We have very respectable people in the part of the ship where we are. We had 200 passengers on board, and 127 of them were in one part together. The Sunday before last there was a woman confined in that part, and we have seen two little children put into the Mighty Deep out of that part of the ship, but our children all seem to enjoy themselves very much and look as fat and fresh as when they left home. When we want little Alfred to get up in the morning the girls tell him his little chickens are on the deck, and then he jumps up to go and feed them.

Now I must try and tell you a little of what we have seen since we have been on the water. We saw nothing on the ocean for a long time except some sea hogs. Last Sunday week we passed what they call Bird Island which was a beautiful sight. It was two immense round rocks out in the main sea all covered with large birds and white with their eggs. In the morning we were on the Banks of Newfoundland and then we saw vessels all round us and fishing smacks. Our boat went out and brought in some fish for breakfast, and our captain gave us a large cod for our dinner. On that day we saw two large whales.

We saw nothing more in the water until we came in sight of land, and then the sight was beautiful to see. The mountains seemed higher than the clouds and we saw the snow lying on the tops of them. The country appeared barren and mountainous until we came nearer to Quebec and then we saw numbers of houses on each side of us, all white ones. Quebec is a beautiful town to look at. We have not been ashore yet but are going in the morning. We expect to proceed to Montreal on Monday.

PART ONE: THE JOURNEY

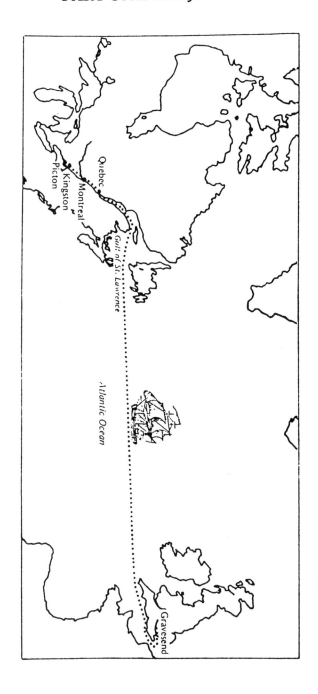

Give my love to Thomas. I hope he will read this letter to his grandmother at Frant and give my love to her and all my sisters, and tell her I will write to her as soon as we are landed and to you again. Tell Thomas and dear Laura that their father joins with me in kindest love to them and please to accept the same yourself from your affectionate son and daughter.

P.S. I forgot to tell you that we saw two boats worked by four pretty little ponies. It looked so pretty to see horses for sailors.

Letter 4

Bloomfield
July 6, 1843

Dear Father and Mother,

We hope these few lines will find you and our dear children in good health as thank God it leaves us out here at present. When we wrote to you last we had just arrived at Quebec. Alfred and I went ashore there on the Sunday. We went to see the Plains of Abraham where the battle was fought, and we saw the Monument that was erected on the spot where General Wolfe was shot. It was a great sight to see the batteries and wagon loads of cannon balls that lay around them.

The steam vessel came and took us on the Monday afternoon at five o'clock and we arrived safe at Montreal on Tuesday about twelve o'clock. There we hired a room for which we gave one shilling and threepence a day. The children and I stopped there and Alfred went down to Brome. He found Brooker and Stevens that went from Frant but not doing so well as he expected and he did not like that part of the country. It was very cold and stoney and could not grow any wheat. It was a hundred miles there and he was gone nearly a week. When he came back we thought we would go further up the country so we took shipping for Kingston which cost us four pounds ten shillings. We were three days and three nights going.

Thomas, your father says I am to tell you that we saw more islands than ever you read of. We went through ninety locks, through little narrow places where there was just room for the vessel to go through between rocks and woods and then out into the wide lakes again. We saw trees tacked together and a fire on them, and a tent that men lived in made of the bark. They floated on the water and they went up and down the river lumbering in the woods in them. We went

PART ONE: THE JOURNEY

to Bytown and we saw the house Colonel By lived in when he was Governor out there.

When we got to Kingston we met an English gentleman who was very kind to us and took us into a storeroom of his. We stopped with them for a week and he advised Alfred to go to a place called Picton about seventy miles from there. Edgar and his father went, and the children and I stopped at Kingston. There another gentleman offered them a house rent-free until Alfred could suit himself to something. So he came back and fetched us all up there to a place called Bloomfield about five miles from Picton. It is fine open country where we are and there are large cultivated farms. The farmers are almost all Quakers.

It seems here that every man must have land before he can do anything for himself. None here will employ a man steadily, only for a few months in the summer and there is no such thing as to get money of them. They will let you have anything they have got except that.

The gentleman whose house we live in has taken Sarah to live with them. She has been there a fortnight and likes it very well. She is to have two dollars a month. Edgar went to a situation yesterday for three months. He is to have seven dollars a month.

Dear Mother if you were here and had got a farm you might ride in your

THE UPPER CANADA COACHES leave
MONTREAL EVERY DAY except
Saturday and *Sunday*, at FOUR o'clock, A. M.
Montreal, May 3, 1832.   d

LAKE ONTARIO.

THE SPLENDID NEW STEAMBOAT
GREAT BRITAIN,
CAPTAIN JOS. WHITNEY,

four wheel carriage, for here they all have a pair of horses, and the wagons and gigs keep continually running all the day long. I will just tell you what they say about here, that 'tis a heaven for women but a bad place for men and horses.

We hope you will write us a long letter when you receive this and send us word how you are getting on and how your crops are. Please tell us how your hops look and how you get on with your dairy. We cannot get any cheese here. The farmers make it and sell it in the fall. Butter is one shilling and sevenpence a pound; meat is very cheap, but clothing is very dear where we are and earthenware is a most extravagant price. We are troubled to get anything to use. We ought to have brought that with us of all things.

We are just as well off as I thought we should be. We have not got a chair or a table or a bedstead belonging to us. Our being obliged to travel so far and getting no employment it has taken all our capital nearly.

Tell dear Laura to send word how many chickens she has got, and accept our kindest love from

Your affectionate son and daughter

Addressed to:

Mr. T. Standen   Post office stamp
Miskins Farm   Lamberhurst, Kent
Ticehurst, Sussex   July 29, 1843
Old England

Letter 5

Written by Alfred Eastwood to Sophia's parents

Picton
November 28, 1843

Dear Father and Mother and Children both,

With pleasure I sit down to write a few lines to you hoping it will find you all in good health as thank God it leaves us at present. I hope Mother continues to have her health still better than when we left her. Our own little children all grow and look fat and well. I don't think you would know Sarah and Ann. They are grown both tall and stout and Edgar the same.

A NEW LIFE IN CANADA

You were kind enough to say you would send me a little money which if you can I should be much obliged to you. You should be sure to have it again when our money at Frant comes due. If you could send me from thirty to forty sovereigns, I should be very glad. If I had forty sovereigns I could get a farm of fifty acres and then I could bring my family up and do well here as there are no taxes to pay, only a few days work to do out on the road. They let the farms in the spring and the out-going tenant takes the crop of wheat that is in the ground and you have it the same when you leave so that you have the first year without wheat and a rent to pay, which makes the first year a hard one. Too many of them want part of the rent when you enter on the land. If you cannot send me more than thirty pounds I must take three acres of land but that is hardly enough for my family.

Here is a gentleman that has offered me thirty acres of land and to employ me in my spare time, but I don't like the soil. It is swampy and not good corn land. Another gentleman has offered to give me my choice of four farms from fifty to one hundred acres of cleared land, each lot for twenty-five pounds a year and I am to do five pounds worth of fencing. They are not many miles from the town of Kingston and situated close to the lakeshore where you can see all the steam vessels on the water, and they are for sale at a very moderate price. One of the farms has as good buildings as they are on Miskins [the farm in England] and a beautiful house with two front parlours and six bedrooms and every other convenience. It has the privilege of clearing more land and selling the cord wood at six shillings per cord to the steamers. Now if Mother and you and our children would come here and bring a few hundreds with you then you might have as nice a place as Miskins and a pair of horses and carriage to ride in and no turnpike to pay or taxes. And Mother, you might live without work.

I will tell you now how the money can be sent. The money must be paid in to the Bank of British North America in London which can be done through any banking house in the country and an order obtained on the branch of the British North America in Kingston, Canada West.

I suppose you would like to know what I am doing now. I have hired myself to a farmer until the first of April to make sure of work through the winter for nine shillings and sixpence a week and my board in the house. So you may see we are not flowing with milk and honey some describe it to be. The price of labour here is two shillings sixpence a day in the winter and three shillings a day in the summer. They give us four shillings a day for haying and five shillings a day for harvesting but the harvesting seldom lasts more than a fortnight. Here no favour is shown to a good workman who goes ahead and does most. A man with a family like mine can hardly live without a little land in this country. If he depends on his work he must hire himself by the year and then he will get from twenty to twenty-five pounds a year with house rent and firewood. He will not get that in money. It will be in provisions and clothes and other produce. It is a good place

PART ONE: THE JOURNEY

for a single man that is steady and working. They will give him as much as a married man and he may soon save money. They work very hard and long days here from sunrise till sunset.

Edgar is living at Mr. Thirtle's house at present and he has thirty shillings a month wages. He looks after one riding horse and waits about the house. It is where Sarah lived when we first came, but she left about a month ago and she is now living in a Quaker's family. She has twelve shillings a month wages.

I must tell you a little news that will surpise you. I have had an offer of marriage for Sarah. A young gentleman came to her mother and me one or two times to ask our consent, but we told him we thought her too young to think of marrying anyone. He wanted us to allow her to be placed under the care of his father and mother until we thought it proper to give our consent that she might not be exposed to any temptation. They are old people living in a large fine house in Picton but he does not live with them. He is brother to Mr. Thirtle and has one sister, a single lady that stops most of her time with Mrs. Thirtle. She was very much taken with Sarah and gave her a present and asked her if she could not fancy her brother. Sarah told her she did not wish to marry anyone yet. She offered her a book for a keepsake with the cover gilted with gold but Sarah would not take it so she gave it to her mother to give to which of her children she pleased. She says if ever she has an opportunity she will send it home to dear little Laura.

The girls want me to tell you they had a sleigh ride on the snow on the 28th of October. But we have no snow at present but a very hard frost. The weather is very clear and cold. There does not seem to be any foggy weather as there is in England.

Little Helen wants me to tell her grandmother and grandfather that she has hemmed a pocket handkerchief and that she has been to the English Church. Edgar has been confirmed by the Bishop at the English Church. You wished us to send word what books were left. Ann left her Bible and two copy books and a cyphering book, and Sophia left her Testament and spelling book and copying book and cyphering book.

Thomas, you wanted to know whether Edgar and I had used our guns much. We have not, for I did not find it as I expected, and I had not much heart for shooting. The rabbits are like one hears at home, and there is great hunting of wild ducks. They go out in boats on the lake to shoot them. I went for half a day and shot five and was like to get shipwrecked. The weather came up rough and we were [blown] in our boat to the trees and could not get out again. Edgar has been several times shooting. We have some deer where we be but not much game. I have seen plenty of partridges in the wild wood.

I will tell you a little of my travels since I have been in America. I took a circle 300 miles on foot into the wild wood. I went first to Wellington and up to Lake Ontario and along beside it for forty miles, through Consecon Lake and then through Brighton. That was a large village, and to Colbourne, and that is a nice village. Then we turned off to Crahme and into the wild wood. That is a new settled place; and I went over the Pine Plains and that is an unsettled place. There were wolves and bears and foxes. I find I have not room to tell you all where I went so your mother will write you all about it.

I had almost forgot to tell you the price of things here that I shall want. A good cow costs five pounds; a good pair of working oxen from twelve to fifteen pounds a dray; a plow, two pounds ten shillings; a new wagon, eighteen pounds. I hope, dear father, you will write by the return of the mail and let me know if you can send me the money and when you expect it will be here. Please direct it to me: Picton Post Office near Kingston, Prince Edward District, Upper Canada, North America.

I must now conclude with our kindest love from your affectionate son and daughter.

Letter 6

Rawdon
June 29, 1844

Dear Father and Mother and Children both,

We are afraid you will think us very ungrateful for not having written to you before, but we have been waiting so that we might tell you about what we are going to do. We have taken 100 acres of wild land and are going right into the heart of the forest. We have taken it on lease for ten years. Our rent will be three pounds a year until we can pay for our land. It is about eleven shillings per acre unless we can pay for it before the ten years are expired and then they will allow some reduction. We received the money you so kindly sent us quite safe and without any trouble which we were very much obliged to you for.

The land that we have taken is called first-rate land. It is very heavily timbered, and Alfred says it is as good soil as ever he saw. He says that he wishes you had all the hop poles and timber that he shall draw in heaps and burn. There are 100 acres joining ours. It is beautiful land. Now if you have a mind to come, Thomas, and learn to swing an axe we will take that for you. They make potash here of their ashes and they say that will pay for clearing the land. We have got a yoke of oxen for which Alfred paid forty-five dollars.

We moved from Picton about a fortnight ago. We are now living about forty-five miles from there but we are not living on our own land yet. Alfred hired a house about eight miles from where we are going. Edgar and his father went back last week and cut a road about two miles into our land where they intend to build the house. Last Monday they both started with their oxen and provision to stop all the week. It is now Friday and I look for them home tonight.

They are coming home tonight to go to a logging bee tomorrow. When they have about fourteen acres chopped people here make a bee and invite all their neighbours. They go there with their teams to work all day and they treat them with vitals and as much whiskey as they like to drink. This bee is close to our house and they expect fifty neighbours there with teams. They will draw the logs together in heaps ready to burn. The women go too, and we are going to quilt a quilt for the woman. When work is done we all enjoy ourselves together.

Rawdon has only been settled a few years but there are great clearings in it and nice houses. It is a good neighbourhood and the people are very friendly. They come every day from somewhere to see me and invite me to come and see them for to get acquainted. They say when we get back in the woods the nearest house will be two miles from us until more settlers come in.

PART ONE: THE JOURNEY

A NEW LIFE IN CANADA

Edgar is very willing to go in the woods with us. He says I am to tell Thomas that he has plenty of partridges and pigeons and hopes soon to shoot one. He lived as hostler at a large inn in Picton in the winter. He earned seven dollars a month beside what he had given to him. They would have given him nine dollars a month if he would have stopped all the year, but his father could not do without him.

Sarah and Sophia are now living nearly fifty miles from us. Sarah lives in an English family and Sophia is living at Bloomfield at a farmhouse. They are Quakers that we became well acquainted with. They keep her and clothe her and will send her to school in the winter. Sarah has not been home a week with us since we have been in the country. Ann is at home. Her feet and ankles swell so that she is not able to hire out. The other children are all well. Little Alfred grows nicely but I am sorry to say does not improve much in his talk.

Our neighbours are going back with your father next week to build us a house. They will build it in one day so that we can go and live in it. I think I can hear you laugh at it, but if we have our life and health it is not such a one as we shall build some day.

I must conclude with kindest love to you all. We hope you will write by the return of the mail. Please direct to us, Rawdon Post Office District, Victoria near Belleville, Canada West, North America.

PART TWO: INTO THE WILDWOOD

Letter 7

Rawdon
December 2, 1844

My dear Father and Mother and Children both,

With pleasure I sit down to answer your kind letter which we did not receive until the second of November. We were very much surprised to hear that your farm [Miskins] was sold. We hope that you got a good price for it, and we wish you every success in your new undertaking.

You wished to know what room I have in our house. I think I can see you laugh when I tell you we have only one room. It is what they call a shanty. All the people here build such when they first go into the woods. We have got it weather-proofed and it is very warm. We have no floor laid yet but your father fetched home the boards for it yesterday. He bought 500 foot of inch board for seven shillings sixpence. One of the oldest farmers who helped build our shanty says it is the best one he ever helped put up.

We have one pair of oxen and one cow. We could keep any quantity of stock if we could buy it, as the woods are beautiful pasture in the summer, and by going a little distance we can cut enough hay for the winter out of the marshes that are along the riverside. We are very much in want of another cow. I hope we shall be able to get one in the spring but I am afraid we shall not.

We have no wheat sown. We have four acres ready for spring wheat and twelve acres more underbrushed ready to chop down this winter. We don't know what we shall be able to get ready to crop as that all depends on the spring. We have laid our ashes up in an ash house ready to make potash in the spring. I will try to tell you what it is. A strong mix is made of the ashes and boiled in a large iron furnace until it becomes thick like pitch. When it is cold it is a hard substance and is put into barrels and sold for twenty-four dollars for 500 weight.

We are in hope that little Alfred improves a little. Little Helen and Eliza grow into nice little girls. We have not heard from Sarah or Sophia since last June. I am in hope that Ann's legs are a little better.

We are happy to hear that dear little Laura makes herself so comfortable. So happy we should be to see you all. Dear Mother, I think you would like America, and if you were to come we could soon build you a house as we have plenty of timber and a sawmill about seven miles off. My dear Thomas, Edgar sends his love to you, and he will write to you in about a month's time and tell you of all the animals we have in the woods.

Our summer here was very wet and we had a great deal of thunder. The first part of harvest was rather wet but very plentiful. Wheat is three shillings sixpence per bushel, and oats one shilling, and peas two shillings.

Our winters here are very long and cold but very healthy, the weather being mostly clear. We had a heavy fall of snow on the 28th and 29th of October, but it went away in a few days and we had pleasant weather for three weeks. But now the ground is covered with snow and we don't expect to see it gone until next March or April. The sun will shine beautiful, bright, and clear and freeze all the time. We have hardly had a cold since we have been here. The people here ride wrapped up in furs in their sleighs and have bells round the horse's belly and neck. In this country the people all harp on the snow coming because of the sleighing.

I hope you will write to us again at the first opportunity. The children all send their love to their grandfather and mother and brother and sister.

Our kindest love to you all

PART TWO: INTO THE WILDWOOD

Letter 8

Rawdon
March 21, 1845

My dear Father and Mother and Children both,

We received your kind letter March 5th and were truly glad to hear that you were all in good health as thank God it leaves us all here at present except Ann. Her ankles, I am sorry to say, are not so well. I think it must be the rheumatics she is troubled with.

I must tell you that Edgar and I have been to Bloomfield to see Sarah and Sophia and I am happy to say that we found them both well and happy. Sarah is grown into quite a woman. She is tall and stouter than I am. We had a very pleasant journey to see them. Edgar stopped one week and I stopped three weeks. They are living about a quarter mile from each other.

You say you think Sophia is too young to be out, but my dear boy she is not treated as the servants are in England. She is just the same as their own child and they sent her to school all this winter. She has been with them a year now and they have given her a lot of nice clothes. She is quite a little Quaker; it is "thee" and "thine" all the time. They both desired their love to you.

When I wrote Sarah said I was to tell her grandmother that she is going to learn to knit and to spin and to weave, as the farmers here all make up their own wool. Sarah is getting three dollars a month wages. There are twelve children where she is and very near another. They keep twelve cows, and there is only Sarah and their own daughter, a girl about her age to do the work.

When we went to Bloomfield we rode four miles over the ice. There is no danger in it here for the ice is frozen three to four feet thick. It is still very cold but we don't know much about it because we always keep a large fire night and day.

We were pleased to hear you, my dear boy were such a farmer. We hope it will please God to send you good luck in all your undertakings and that you will be diligent and look after it [the farm]. We were very glad to hear that Mother and dear little Laura like their new home so well. We hope that Father does also. Dear Mother, we cannot promise when we can come to dinner with you so we will be content to take such as you have got when we come.

You were so kind to enquire what a cow would cost us. It will cost from four to five pounds. Now it is spring and little Helen sends her love to her grandfather. A hen will cost one shilling. She is so delighted about it, I think it is never out of her head.

Alfred has not been to any bank to know if a note would go here but he enquired of the postmaster. He told him he had no doubt but it would be just as good as gold if he was sure it was pure, but there was so much forgery in this country it made people case what they took. But we have banks and cashiers in Belleville so that we could get any kind changed without any expense to us. We should be very glad of it if you could send it, but we don't wish you to put yourselves out too much to do it as we will try to get along in the best way we can.

Edgar sends his love to you, Thomas, and says he will write you a long letter soon. Ann sends her love to you all and little Alfred says his grandfather is going to send him his little Aldeny cow.

Our kindest love to you both my dear children and please accept the same my dear Father and Mother from your affectionate son and daughter.

A NEW LIFE IN CANADA

Letter 9

Rawdon
July 21st, 1846

Dear Father and Mother and Children All,

I have written these few lines which I hope will find you all in good health. Alfred has had a very bad cold which made him quite sick but he is better now. We were truly sorry to hear that Mother had been so ill. We hope and trust that she is better by this time.

Edgar says I am to tell you how he spent his time in the winter. He went chopping down timber all the day long with about twenty men, English and Irish and Scotch and at night there was some singing, some dancing, some reading. They had two blankets to wrap around them and the soft side of a plank to sleep on. That was how he passed two of the coldest months last winter.

Alfred says that I am to give his love to his father and mother and tell them he is not quite so young as he used to be. He is getting quite grey-headed, but he has his health much better than he did in England.

I must tell you a little about our farming now. We have got five acres of fall wheat, and it is very good. We have this day begun to cut it. We have four acres of spring wheat. Three acres of it is very good. It all came good but we had frosts so late and so severe that it killed it out in patches in one acre. There we dragged in oats, so there are oats and wheat together. We have about two acres of oats, and they are pretty good, and about an acre and a half of meadowland. We had a fine lot of timothy grass on it this year. We have corn that looks first rate, some buckwheat, and a piece of new land with potatoes. The ground will all be planted with crops in the spring so that then we shall have twenty acres cleared and fenced. If Edgar and his father are spared they think of getting ten acres chopped this winter.

We have only got one cow, one yoke of cattle, a twelve-month bull, and a heifer calf with our cow. We have six nice hogs and four pigs. They just get their living in the woods all the time. The trees are loaded with beechnuts this year so they will come in fat.

My dear Thomas, your father says he has been thinking a great deal about your farm and he thinks you cannot make it answer. He does not know your circumstances, but if your business is likely to go wrong with you, you had better give it right up and come to Canada. If you have only fifty pounds when you get to us you could get a farm. A yoke of cattle would be all the team you would want at first. He doesn't wish to persuade you by no means to leave your grandfather and mother, but he thinks you had better all come.

Dear Father and Mother, Alfred says here is a nice farm of one hundred acres about three miles from Front Rawdon with between seventy and eighty acres of good cleared land and well fenced with a new frame barn and stable and granary. It is all in one building. Alfred says he could buy you that and get a good deed of it for two hundred pounds. There is no house on it. The farmer lives in a shanty. The putting up of a good frame house would cost about forty pounds. It would bear as good crops as Miskins and be as pleasant a place to live.

At Front Rawdon there is a fine large stone grist mill, a carding mill, and four large stores. We don't carry our sugar or molasses anywhere to market. We use all that at home, but those who do sell it get five to sixpence a pound. Tell Mother I have just been making soap for the first time and have made a nice lot, enough to last me all the year.

Please give our love to dear Laura and Thomas and his wife. I hope she is safe through her trouble by this time, and dear Father and Mother please accept kindest love from your affectionate son and daughter.

Letter 10

Rawdon
December 2nd, 1846

My dear Father, Mother, Children both,

We have been very anxiously waiting to hear from you as we thought you would be sure to have written to us before now. Little Helen and Edgar both had the fever and ague this fall but they soon got better. There has been a great deal of sickness round about us this fall. Alfred very much wishes to know how his mother's health is and how you like living at Rotherfield and also how Thomas gets on with farming. We hear it is very hard times in England. Send us word if it be true.

We had a beautiful harvest here and our crops were very good. We grew a nice lot of wheat. Alfred says we shall have plenty for ourselves to use and he will have grown eighty to a hundred bushels to sell besides other grain. I think I told you when I wrote to you before that our potatoes were not looking so well, but they came on and we grew a nice lot. Alfred is gone to bespeak him a new cleaning machine. He is going to build a little place to put his grain in the dry, and he will have a threshing machine and thresh it all out. He has not threshed or sold any yet. We make potash of our ashes for what money we have had. We are in hopes we shall get along very comfortably in Canada.

Edgar has just come in. He has been gone out about two hours with his gun and he has brought in a fine fat buck, so if you will come to dinner with us on Christmas day, we will give you some roast turkey and venison and plum pudding.

Tell little Laura her father and I both send our love to her, and send us word when you write if she ever wishes to come to America. We received a letter from my brother in the summer. He informed us we were grandfather and mother in England but I am in hopes that there is no sign of it in America.

We had a very hot dry summer here, but we have had a great deal of rain this fall and the roads are quite unpassable, but the winter appears to be setting in now. It is very cold and frosty and we have snow on the ground.

We hope, dear Father and Mother, you will write to us when you receive this by return of post as we think it so long since we heard from you. We must conclude now and remain your affectionate son and daughter.

P.S. I forgot to tell you we have got five nice fat hogs to kill.

PART TWO: INTO THE WILDWOOD

Postscript from Edgar to Thomas:

Thomas, you were bragging not long ago of being a farmer. I have commenced now. You commenced in the English fields with a wife, horses and cows; I have begun with a little yoke of bulls and an axe in the American woods on a larger scale than you. I will write you a good long letter very soon. I would have written you one before but I have had so much work to do and so many pretty girls to go and see, I really haven't had time.

> I remain your affectionate brother
> Edgar Eastwood

A NEW LIFE IN CANADA

Letter 11

Rawdon
March 10, 1847

Dear Father and Mother and Children all,

With great pleasure we received your kind letter and we were very glad to hear you were all well. Edgar had a bad misfortune about two months ago and he cut his foot with his axe very bad. He has not done a day's work since, but it is nearly well now. We received a letter from Sophia about a fortnight ago. Sarah and she are both still living together at Bloomfield. They have both got the whooping cough. Sophia goes to school this winter.

Dear Father we were all highly delighted to hear that you talk of making us a visit, and we hope you will not disappoint us. Little Alfred and Helen and Eliza are all alive and jumping at the thoughts of Grandfather coming. They say that when the warm weather comes they shall go every day to the bottom of the lane to meet their Grandfather. How happy we should all be to see you.

Now dear Father, I will commence to tell you a straight road to come to us. You would of course go to London to take your passage and you must hire it to Quebec or Montreal. It makes but little difference which, only if you wish to stop a day or two in Quebec you had better hire a passage to that place as you must travel by steamer when you get there, and you can come to Montreal any day from there. If you hire your passage from London to Montreal, when you get to Quebec the steamboat will come along the side of the ship and take you right forward. When you get to Montreal there will be plenty of people to tell you where to go to the wharf to take your passage to Kingston, which is about three days journey. When we came, for a single person the fare was fifteen shillings, but we hear that it is much cheaper now. When you get to Kingston you must take your passage to Belleville. You will be only twenty-seven miles from us.

You must put a letter in the post for us to say when you leave England and put another in for us when you get to Montreal, and then we will watch the post office. Alfred says he shall be happy to come to Belleville to meet you, but should you come to Belleville unknown to us you must enquire your way to Fiddlers Mills at Front Rawdon. You would almost any day find teams coming to Front Rawdon by enquiring at the shops and inns. When you get to Front Rawdon you will be eleven miles from us and then you must enquire your way to our settlement which is four miles farther. When you get there any of the people will know where we are living.

PART TWO: INTO THE WILDWOOD

When you are hiring with the steamboats you must have a good look out and not pay them all they ask you, and you must at all times keep an eye on your luggage or you will lose it. If you don't come in the cabin you must be sure to bring your own provisions as you would not like the ship's board unless you come in the cabin. If you bring your provisions, good hams and cheese are the best things you would like, with a little pickle and some hard biscuits such as Mother can make at home, and a little hard bread. You can have good bread to last for three weeks and a little prepared barley. Coffee you will like better than tea, and some brandy and a little keg of cider, if you have it, will be good when you get out to sea if you should feel sick.

Dear Father, Alfred will thank you to bring him a real good strong handbill and a hay cutter and a goose neck spud, not a heavy one for hop digging but a light one for dung. He doesn't mind it having the handle being in it if it will come better without it. Now we shall quite expect you will come and we hope and trust you will not disappoint us.

Thomas, we were very glad to hear that your farm has paid its way, and we hope it will continue to do so. We were very much obliged to you for the flower seeds, and when I get some pretty ones I will send them home.

You want to know what Stephen [Alfred's brother] could do here. If he came here and had no money and hired out by the year he could get twenty-five pounds per year, and house rent and firewood and his own board. His three boys would get just as much, and if he works by the day he could get two shillings sixpence; and in haying, four shillings a day; and in harvest, five shillings per

41

day with board all the time. But we don't wish to persuade him to leave his home for he will find some hardships here.

Dear Mother, I have put you in a few musk melon seeds. They grow very fine here, as large as a quart pot, and are beautiful to eat. They are quite yellow when ripe. Just cut them and pare them and scrape their insides out, and they are the nicest fruit I ever tasted. You must plant them as you do cucumbers and at the same time in the most sunny place you can find.

Wheat here is four shillings ninepence per bushel; oats, one shilling threepence per bushel; India corn, two shillings sixpence; potatoes, one shilling sixpence per bushel. There is a great scarcity of potatoes here in some places, and not more than fifty miles from us they are selling for four shillings a bushel.

Edgar has been home with us ever since we have been farming, except sometimes for a week or two, but he is going to work for himself on his father's farm this spring.

My dear son, I was pleased to hear your little daughter was called Sophia. You must give her a kiss for her grandmother.

Kindest love from your
Affectionate son and daughter

Letter 12

This letter was written by Thomas Mann, an Agricultural Society agent who had recently emigrated from Sussex, England. He called on the Eastwoods at the request of Sophia's father.

Toronto, Upper Canada
September 25th, 1847

My dear Sirs,

Agreeable to your request I beg to say I called on Mr. Eastwood of Rawdon. After some little difficulties I found them out, but I must tell you I missed my road and went about seven miles out of my way. Therefore I did not get there the same day I ought to have done, having all that distance to come back and it being somewhat a lonely road. I went through the bush as they call it, for about ten miles and never saw anyone, not even a house or a shanty. I saw footmarks of the wolves but never saw one. I was there on the 22nd of August. I stayed there for about five days. I found them all well, with the exception of Mrs. Eastwood. She was very poorly with the fever and ague. I found them tolerable comfortable and getting pretty well seasoned to the bush.

PART TWO: INTO THE WILDWOOD

The situation is such that I would not recommend you to come there to reside. I believe they get a very good living; as for comforts, it is quite out of the question in this country. I had the pleasure of sleeping in a shanty there for the first time. You might find a worse place than that in England. It is a substantially built one. It's build with logs just hewed up, and the top is the same only hollowed out and laid one over the other something similar to a trough; therefore, the water runs off from the top.

They have got about thirty acres of the land chopped in all, about twenty in cultivation last year. The soil is very good, most of it. Some is rather stoney, a very good lime stone. He [Alfred] expects to have all the thirty acres in this next year, which he calculates on getting about 200 bushels from. His oats and peas were good. He was busy harvesting when I was there.

We carry corn and hay in the bush in this country on jumpers. It is not fixed on wheels, but slides along the ground. The ends are crooked up so as to prevent it catching hold of stones or stumps. They use oxen in the bush. Horses would be but little service to them. It looked something strange to me first coming out to see the stumps standing all over the fields. It takes some years for them to rot in the ground.

I must tell you what stock he has. He has a yoke of oxen, two cows, two yearling steers, one yearling heifer, and two weaning calves, and six or eight hogs; therefore, he will have plenty of pork. His pasture for his cattle is very extensive. I don't know how much, but some thousands of acres. Anyone may keep plenty of stock in the summer in the bush, but it is difficult to find them sometimes. Hogs and all run in this country.

I cannot say I fancy this country altogether. It's all very well for anyone to talk about it but you can form no idea without seeing it. I have travelled a great deal in the back woods of Canada. I have sometimes got in a log house and sometimes in a shanty. Anyone will give you a night's lodging and a breakfast in the morning if you are travelling. Sometimes I dropped in with decent sort of folks and some very indifferent ones.

I believe the wheat crop in America is very indifferent some places. They don't get more than ten or twelve bushels per acre. There is some complaint about the potatoes rotting about here. Wheat is fetching now about three shillings sixpence sterling. That is about four shillings threepence currency. An English shilling here is worth one shilling threepence. It is pretty much all English money in Canada.

I thought of writing you last mail, but I was unwell with what they call the summer complaint, which is very common in this country. I have but little time to spare as the mail closes this morning for all English letters. It is sooner than I expected by two or three days. I have not heard from home yet, but I expect a letter this day as the mail is expected in.

I will never persuade anyone to come here, as the climate and the ways

are so very different. I suppose you heard when I landed by my friends on the 27th July. I saw your granddaughters at Bloomfield. They were quite well and desired to be kindly remembered to you all. I should feel obliged if you will have the kindness to let my friends know I am quite well. As soon as I hear from them I will write to them by the next mail which is about a fortnight. Please give my kind love to them all.

I find in this country people want to be here awhile before they enter into anything. Toronto is a business place. I would have written more but have not time. With kind respects to all,

Yours truly,
Thomas A. Mann

PART TWO: INTO THE WILDWOOD

Letter 13

Rawdon
May 9th, 1849

My dear Father and Mother and Children both,

I hope these few lines will find you all in good health as thank God it leaves us all here at present. I mentioned Alfred's illness to you in my last letter. He seems to be quite recovered of that, though he says he doesn't feel so strong as he did before. It has been pretty hard times with us this year. The doctor's bills have been very heavy on us, but we shall get along if it pleases God to keep his [Alfred's] health and send us good crops.

Alfred has just done putting in spring wheat. That is all our dependence this year as he was not able to sow any fall wheat, only a small piece that got in after Edgar came home. Edgar has married now and has to have a living. His father and he are partners so he will receive half of what they can raise this year.

A NEW LIFE IN CANADA

Edgar's wife has got a nice little son, and we are going to have his name Thomas.

We have had a pretty good sugar year. I have made 112 pounds of sugar and ten gallons of molasses. We have had a very cold winter. The spring opened early but the weather continued very cold and freezes hard every night. We have no signs of green leaves yet.

Mr. Buckland is living in Toronto in the Agricultural Society, and Thomas Mann is travelling for him to get members to join it. I think dear Father and Mother, you might come and make us a visit for we have an old gentleman close by us that came out here last spring to see his sons. He is seventy years old. He is going back again the last of this month and he says that he shall come back here again. He comes from the west of England.

Give my love to my sister Wickens. I will tell her how I make my soap. When we kill our hogs we kill them all in one day. Then we take their innards and pick the fat off them and wash them. Then we take lye strong enough to bear an egg and boil it. It turns into soap as thick as jelly. Then we fill it up with weak lye until the grease has all gone off the top. One pound of good grease will make a pail full of soap. We save all the bacon rinds and all the fowl grease for soap. When we make hard soap we put in a little rosin and salt. When it is cold we cut it out in bars.

Things are selling very low here. Wheat is three shillings sixpence per bushel, and oats are one shilling. We have got a new school house built about a mile from us, so I am in hopes that another year the children will be able to go to school. I must now conclude for Edgar is waiting to take my letter to the post office. So my dear friends we must bid you all farewell for this time. Please to give our love to Laura and to Thomas. We sincerely hope he has had good crops this year and that he is more attentive to his business, and please accept the same dear Father and Mother.

46

PART TWO: INTO THE WILDWOOD

Letter 14

Rawdon
September 22nd, 1849

Dear Father and Mother and Children both,

With great pleasure we received your kind letter. We began to think you had forgotten us altogether. We are much obliged to you for the things you sent us by Thomsett. We have not got them yet but we received a letter from Bloomfield the same day we received yours to say that Thomsett was safe there, and the things you sent.

I must tell you a little news. Our daughter Sarah has married and gone about 200 miles from us. She has married a young man about twenty-two years of age. His name is Richard Morden. He was bred and born at Bloomfield and is considered a very sober and industrious young man. His father sold a cleaned farm at Bloomfield and has moved his family to a newly settled part of Upper Canada where he has bought twelve hundred acres of land, and Sarah and Richard have gone with them. I have not seen her since she has been married, but she writes that she is well pleased with her new situation.

Our little Helen is going to Bloomfield this fall to live at Mr. Noxen's. Mrs. Noxen wishes to have her that she may be company for Sophia. They will send her to school this winter.

Thomas stated in his letter that Laura had a wish to come to America which we were delighted to hear. If you are willing to part from her we shall be most happy to receive her. I don't know of any part of the family that is likely to come home, but her father will come to any part of America to meet her if you can get a chance to send her out. About her coming, you must let her have a nice little light feather bed with her and a chest of drawers to pack her clothes in. Ann says I am to tell her that will be a marriage portion for her when she gets here, for all the young men expect the girls to have a feather bed and a chest of drawers.

Edgar's wife is an English girl. Her name was Susan Neal. His little boy grows nicely and is quite a little pet among us. They are going to live by themselves this fall. We had a bee about two months ago. There were nearly forty men and several teams and they raised Edgar a log shanty the same day. It is in one of our fields. He is to have fifty acres of his father's land if he can pay for it.

We have had a very hot and dry summer here, but Alfred says I am to tell

you he cannot complain of his crops this year. The wheat is very good and so are the oats, peas, India corn, potatoes, and buckwheat. And we have a nice piece of swedes. He says I am to tell you our stock is increasing. He has got fifteen head of stock now. We have four nice cows and three yoke of cattle, and steers and heifers. Edgar has one cow and one yoke of cattle, and we have eight large hogs, eight sheep, and six pigs.

Thomas, we were sorry to hear your crops were so bad last year. We sincerely hope they are better this. I hope you will write to us again soon and tell us how many children you have and how my little granddaughter Sophia goes on. And I want you to try and write a little plainer for me. I see your writing so seldom I am troubled to read it, dear boy. I was very sorry to hear of the death of my poor brother. I am sure it will be a great trouble to his wife and family.

Edgar and his wife send their love. Ann and the little girls do the same. We remain your affectionate son and daughter.

Letter 15

Rawdon
June 29, 1851

Dear Father and Mother and Children,

With much pleasure I sit down to answer your kind letter written October the 30th, which we received quite safe. We were truly happy to hear you were all well, Mother excepted. We sincerely hope she may be enjoying good health at this time as thank God it leaves us all here at present. I think this is a very healthy part of the country, where Alfred has his health far better than he ever did in England. We were surprised to hear that you were gone to Horse Grove to live now. We want to know if you have got that farm or only live in the house. We were glad to hear your crops were good last year.

We hope Thomas had good luck in selling his hops. You wished to know if we grew any. We do not; only a few for our own use. I have five or six hills along the bottom of the garden. They do not grow quite so large as they do in England, and they do not have any seeds. There is no hop garden near us, but there is one on this side of Belleville about twenty-six miles from us belonging to an Englishman, and I believe he makes a great deal of money of them. Old Mr. Miels that came out here when we did has a hop garden at Bloomfield, and last year he cleared fifty pounds, when all his expenses were paid, from one acre.

49

A NEW LIFE IN CANADA

The things you were so kind as to send by John Thomsett we got quite safe. The chest he took care of. It was not soiled one bit. The box he said was an old one and got broken, and he put the dress and little handkerchiefs with his clothes. The little dress pattern you sent in your letter, Little Eliza says I am to tell her granmama, she has put in her patch work. The spud and hay cutter, Alfred is very much pleased with. The saddle and bridle we have not got, but Mr. Thomsett brought it safe to Bloomfield and left it at Mr. Noxen's.

You wished us to send you word how we get along in this country. Thank God we get along very comfortably. We had good crops last year, good wheat and potatoes, first rate peas, and our crops look beautiful this year. We have about fourteen acres of wheat that looks first rate, and all the spring crops look good. We have had a great deal of rain and fine growing showers.

Edgar has twelve acres of wheat all looking well, and he has two nice cows and one yoke of oxen, one year-old steer, two yearlings and one calf, and two sweet little boys, Thomas and Edgar, and I believe another on the road.

Prices here are very low: wheat, three shillings nine pence per bushel; oats, one shilling sixpence per bushel; peas, two shillings sixpence; India corn, two shillings threepence; potatoes, one shilling threepence; pork, ten dollars per barrel. We have two yolk of cattle, four cows, three heifers, one bull, nine sheep,

one horse, eleven hogs, twenty hens, two geese, one gander.

I must tell you a little about the girls. We received a letter from Sarah last week. They were all well, and she desired her love to her grandmother and grandfather and her brother and sisters. She sent me a lock of her little Susan Emily's hair, and I have enclosed it for her great grandmama. Sophia and Helen are still at Mr. Noxen's at Bloomfield. Helen went to school in the winter. Their father went down with his horse-sleigh and fetched them home for a visit, and the sleighing went away and they stopped a month with us. Then there came another heavy fall of snow and their father took them home. It was in February they came. We had a very sharp, cold winter and a great deal of snow.

We have Ann, Alfred, and Eliza at home. Alfred grows very tall but doesn't improve much in his understanding. Ann and Eliza are going down to Bloomfield to see their sisters. If all is well they are to start the day after tomorrow. They will go down in the steamboat from Belleville. Little Eliza is really delighted with the thought of her journey. You will be glad to hear that we have an English church service here. We have an English gentleman sent by the Colonial Service. He has bought a farm adjoining ours and preaches at our place once a fortnight. Last Tuesday fortnight we had the Reverend Mr. Blonsdell from Trent Church to baptize the children around the settlement, and our place was chosen for the ceremony. He baptized fifteen children and on Wednesday last he came back and baptized six more. He stopped all night at our place and took supper and breakfast each time with us.

Tell dear Laura we would be most happy to see her. We are very much disappointed that no opportunity has offered for her to come. Give our kindest love to Thomas and his wife and dear little children. We hope he will find time to write a few lines to us himself when you receive this. I must tell you that we are going to spin our own wool and make our own flannel this year for the first time.

Alfred joins with me in kindest love to our children and his dear mother, and believe us to remain dear Father and Mother

Your Affectionate Son and Daughter

PART THREE:
AT HOME IN UPPER CANADA

Letter 16

[This letter was written in 1857. The Eastwoods have now lived in Upper Canada for fourteen years.]

Rawdon
August 2, 1857

My dear Daughter:

We received your kind letter about three weeks after its date and I am afraid you will think that I have been very neglectful in not answering it before this time. It gives me great comfort when I receive a letter from you, but oh we should all be so glad to see you.

I must tell you Sarah has just lost her baby. It was a little boy about six months old. He was named after both his grandfathers, Alfred Standen. It is a great grief to Sarah and Richard as they thought so much of their little son, but they should not grieve for him for he is better off than he could ever be on this earth. Ann is stopping with them yet. I think I told you she went home with them last fall, and I look for her home soon. They are about 250 miles from us.

You wished to know the name of the railroad. It is called the Grand Trunk Railroad, and anyone might pay their passage in England to come to Belleville, twenty-seven miles from us. Then there are stages that run from there to Stirling [formerly Front Rawdon] and from Stirling to Marmora. They pass within one mile of our place.

You wished to know if this was a good country for millers. Your father and brother think it is first rate. It is good for either master or man. A good miller gets great wages here. You said had we many English near us? We have. There are English and Irish and Scotch, and every other sort in this country mixed up together.

Our minister is an English man. His name is Gander and he came from Sussex. This is Sunday and Helen and Eliza and Alfred are just starting off to meeting. They said when they went out of the door they wished you were here to go with them. They said I was to tell you they have new bonnets this summer trimmed with white ribbon.

We are busy haymaking. Your father has a great deal of hay this year.

52

PART THREE: AT HOME IN UPPER CANADA

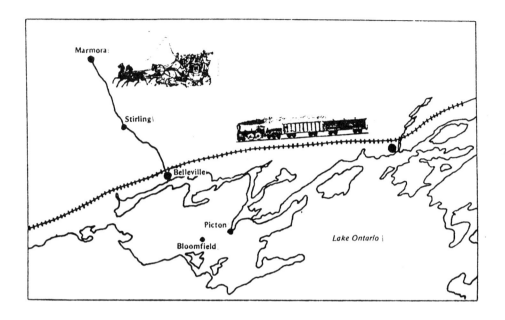

He has had a man between two and three weeks to help him. He has to pay him five shillings a day and his board. Next week they will commence harvest and then the men will get seven shillings six pence per day for cradling the grain and their board. The crops around us are all looking fine. We have had very abundant rains this summer and all the spring crops look beautiful.

We have seven cows. They make us plenty of work but we don't make cheese. We got eleven pence per pound for butter this summer. The cows get their living out in the woods all the summer. We have a large bell on them so that early in the morning you hear it for two miles. Young stock get fat by the fall.

Edgar commenced butchering last winter and he has made a good deal of money by it. He kills meat at his own place and carries it to Marmora. I must tell you what a loss he had this spring. He built a large frame driving shed, stable, and granary. He had the roof on and shingled and the gable ends done when there came a high wind and it blew the building down. It cost him about sixty dollars, but he has got it up again and finished it off.

I hope, my dear girl, you will write again soon. We are all so glad to hear you are so comfortable. Give your father's and my kindest love to your grandfather and accept the same from your ever affectionate father and mother.

A NEW LIFE IN CANADA

Letter 17

Rawdon
February 16th, 1860

My dear Son and Daughter:

With great pleasure I write these few lines to you in answer to your kind letter. I hope your dear little boy runs alone by this time. I hope my dear Laura you do not think that I minded paying for your likeness [photograph] because I told you what it cost. I would not part with it for ten times what it cost. Your father scolds me for telling you. I think your father will have his taken when we go where we can get it done. I think we can have them taken without a frame and sent to you in a letter. We have received all the papers lately you have sent us and are much obliged to you for them. When you write again send me word if you ever receive any from us.

You say your grandfather tells you our house is made of trees. It's what we call a log house. The logs are cut straight and the corners are laid square and even. They are not plastered with mud but good lime mortar and the logs are all hewed flat and smooth inside. We whitewash and paper our rooms and they look very nice. I have three rooms downstairs, a nice large room that we live in and two bedrooms off it. Your father and I sleep in one, and the other we have for a spare room. We have a nice chamber upstairs where we can put all we want. The girls and Alfred sleep up there. We have four large sash windows and two smaller ones. We have a good cellar.

The house looks very pleasant in the summer. It stands a little way off the road. We have lots of roses and lilacs round the house and a flower garden in front and locust trees round about. They are like your laburnum only their flowers are white. We have to raise most of our flowers from seeds because the hard winters kill them. We have a cooking stove that stands out in the room and pipes that go along and up through the chamber. It makes the house very warm all over. Our rooms are all boarded here. We have no brick floors. The farm houses here in the old settlement are a great deal more grand than they are in England.

I will tell you what we keep. We have six cows, twenty-three yearling heifers, and two two-year-old heifers to come in this spring; so if we have good luck I shall have ten cows this summer and one pair of oxen, three yearlings, fifteen sheep, and one horse and four hogs. We have killed six hogs. We have a light one-horse wagon that we ride in the summer and a heavy one that we use on the farm, and a nice sleigh that we ride in the winter. I am thankful to say your father's crops were all good this last year.

Edgar's wife has a young son two weeks old. His little girl was one year and one week old when he was born. They have eight children now. I will tell you what their names are. Thomas and Edgar, Eliza-Sophia, Sarah, Helen, Alfred Tilly, John Standen, and Isaac. Isaac is the baby. Your sister Morden [Sarah] has three children named Susan Emily, Sophia Emily, and Mary Helen.

Edgar butchers when he can get a chance. He likes to do that better than to farm. Your father says he makes off with more than he gets, he is away from home so much. He is a great hand to go ahead. I don't know how he will come out at last.

My pen writes so badly I am afraid you will be troubled to read what I have written. Your brothers and sisters send their kindest love to you and Christopher and to their grandfather. Your father joins me in kindest love to you all.

Letter 18

Rawdon
July 15, 1860

My dear Son and Daughter,

I hope these few lines will find you all in good health. I would have written before but I waited to get the likeness taken which I have sent to you, and your sister Ann has sent you hers. When your father and I had ours taken we took Ann's likeness along and had this taken from that. I don't think it looks quite so good as the one she sent herself, for it looks a little too heavy and dark, but it is a very correct likeness of her. Everyone that has seen your father and I say we look as natural as life. You must have them put in frames because to handle them would spoil the likeness. You must be careful not to get finger marks on them, but take them edgeways. You must show them to your aunts when you have got them fixed.

My flower seeds you sent me grow nicely. The wall flowers and the little white flower with the purple spot are out in blossom now. I hope you will save me some seed of any that you think are pretty. We got your last paper yesterday. We get one every month and are much obliged to you for them. They are very interesting to us to read. I will post you one with this letter. If you get it you will read a description of our Stirling Village. That is what we used to call Front Rawdon. Tell Christopher just to notice what splendid mills we have here. We have all our wheat ground in the Stirling Mill.

All sorts of crops look well here. We have had a very wet season here this summer, but it has been very fine for a few days. We are busy haymaking now. We have lots of fruit this year such as strawberries, raspberries, currants, plums, and some apples, but our orchard doesn't do well. The trees keep dying. Our plum trees are so loaded, we are obliged to prop the limbs up. I had almost forgotten to tell you that I have been to Bloomfield to visit Sophia. I was gone nine days from home. I had a very pleasant journey. I think perhaps Sophia will be married this fall, but I am not sure. Helen sends her love to you. She says she will send you her likeness some day. Kindest love to you and Christopher from

Your affectionate father and mother

Letter 19

Rawdon
November 16, [1863]

My dear Son and Daughter,

I am afraid you will think me very neglectful in not writing to you before but believe me my dearest child it was not for want of thought for you that I did not write. Something would occur and I would put it off. But I hope you will forgive me and not do as I have done, for nothing gives me so much pleasure as to hear from you.

      Edgar's health is not good at the best of times. He had a bad misfortune the last of June. His horse shied at something and threw him. It broke his collarbone and dislocated his shoulder. He has not been able to use his arm all the summer. He just begins to use his hand some, but I am afraid he will never be able to raise his arm again.

      I got a letter from Thomas last week. They were both well. He is on a farm that he rented for two years. He says they had a long drought and their crops were poor. He says that he thinks he will come back to Canada after another year.

      Sarah and her children left us the last of January. Your father and I went with them to Bloomfield. They stopped two weeks with Sophia and Horace and then went up the country. She has built herself a little new house in the Front Street of Walkerton with a shop front. She intends to be milliner and dressmaker. She gave 150 dollars for the eighth of an acre. It has taken almost all her money but I hope it will be better in the end than having rent to pay. She has rented her farm. We had a letter from her a short time back. She said her health had been quite good this summer. She said the times were dull up there and she had not done much work.

The war in the States makes hard times in Canada. It spoils our markets. Nothing that farmers have to sell fetches much, and what we have to pay is very dear. Very poor white cotton such as we used to pay fivepence a yard for is a shilling and fifteen pence, and the printed cottons are from one shilling to one shilling and sixpence per yard.

Helen has another little son. He was born on the 12th of September. He is a sweet pretty baby. They are going to call him Ernest after your dear little son. Little Alfred Gander is a sweet child. I think he is a match for your dear little boy. He seems to know so much.

I have not had a chance to get Alfred and Eliza's likeness taken. This summer the man was gone from Stirling. I hear that he is coming back. If so I will have it done.

Your sister Ann has sent you a small token of her love. It is a book mark that she got from the Crystal Palace at Kingston. She went and made Sophia a visit and stayed nearly a month with them. Sophia and Horace and Ann went to Kingston to the Provincial Show. They had a really pleasant time. They stayed three days in Kingston. They went to see the penitentiary where there were over 800 convicts. Then they got a pass and went through all the barracks and forts. Ann says I am to tell you it was a great sight. She enjoyed herself very much.

I daresay you often wonder what we are all doing. I will tell you what we are doing today. Your father is plowing and Ann has gone to see Helen. Alfred is chopping firewood and Eliza is sewing. We are expecting every day now to have the ground freeze up. It is very mild just now but we have had some very hard frost and some snow. I have nice stocks from the seed you sent me. I have taken them into the house for fear the winter should kill them.

There has been a bad fever a few miles from us. It has taken a great many away. The doctors say it is nearly as bad as the Yellow Fever.

We received a paper from you yesterday for which we are very much obliged. It seems so nice to read the home news. I hope you will write as soon as you receive this. Helen and Joseph both send their kindest love to you and Christopher. Your brothers and sisters all unite in kindest love to you both, and Father joins with me in love to you both and dear little Alfred. Tell him how his Granma would like to see him. I must conclude, and believe us to remain your affectionate father and mother.

I wish you all a Merry Christmas and a Happy New Year.

A NEW LIFE IN CANADA

Letter 20

Rawdon
September 9th, 1864

My dearest Daughter and Son,

I was this day looking at your last kind letter and find it dated May. How swift the time pases away, never to be recalled. I have had so much work this summer that I had very little leisure time.

Eliza's husband came home from the States about two months ago and he has been helping your father do his haying and harvest work. Now he is building a frame shed for your father. I suppose it will be about three weeks before he will have it done. Then he is going to open his blacksmith shop again about a mile and a half from us. I dread to have Eliza leave me. She has always been a dutiful good girl to her father and me. I feel that I can hardly give her up. Her baby is eleven months old today. She is a sweet pretty little child. They have christened her Sophia May Eliza. Ann is still with Sarah. I don't know whether she will come home this winter or not, so when Eliza is gone I shall be quite alone except for Alfred. I don't know what we should do without him, poor fellow. He is so good about doing anything we want him to.

You will have seen by the paper what trouble we have had here with the Fenians, and I am afraid it is not over. But I hope the Almighty will be on our side and save our country and homes from all such lawless ruffians.

Edgar is away to Montreal to see how the markets are. He and another man have been buying up cattle. He is a great speculator, but I am afraid he doesn't make much. His family is all home. His oldest son stands six feet high. This is Monday. Edgar came home last night from Montreal. He is not very well today.

I received a nice letter from Thomas' wife a short time ago and Helen got one last week. She said Thomas had been very ill with a fever for three weeks, but he was better then. I think she is a very pious good woman. I wish his children were safe under her care, but I am afraid they would not like to be controlled now they are got so old. I often hear from Sophia. I think she is very comfortable in her new home though they have not had very good luck with crops since they have been there; but she says they are not discouraged whilst they have their health. She has another little daughter about six months old.

I have put in a little piece of flannel like what we made our dresses from last winter. The piece of cloth is called full cloth. That is what your father and Alfred wear. It is our own make. The flannel is made on cotton warp because all-wool is too heavy. We always use flannel sheets in the winter. We make some white and some streaked with large mixed streaks of black and white sheep wool. They look very nice, and they are so comfortable in this cold country. We don't know what it is to get into a cold bed, although it will be so piercing cold out.

Helen's little Augustine runs alone. Joseph and she both send their love to you both. Joseph has to go to college next week. If all is well he will not be back before Christmas. We are all so sorry to part from him. Helen says she is going to write to you soon.

Butter has been ninepence a pound here all the summer. I have been packing mine nearly all the summer, and I have got about 300 weight by me to sell this fall. I think I shall get from tenpence to a shilling a pound for it.

We have a nice lot of apples this year. We dry our apples here and stew them up for use. Raspberries grow wild here, large and fine as the tame ones do in England. We scald them up in sugar and dry them in the sun. We never think to set our table here for company without preserves or stewed fruit. I must tell you how we save our cucumbers for pickles. We put them in a barrel and cover them with salt and water. When we use them we scald them and put them in vinegar and a little pepper so that we can have pickles every meal if we like.

Your father is calling to know if my letter is ready so I must bid you good-bye.

Letter 21

Rawdon
June 27th, 1869

My dearest Son and Daughter,

We received your very kind letter and were so glad to hear you were all well. This is Sunday and your father and I are quite alone. He is gone upstairs to take a sleep. We have Edgar's second daughter living with us, and she and Alfred have just run over to Edgar's. He lives just one field from us.

Edgar is quite a jobber. He buys and sells and butchers and takes meat to Blairton twice a week. It is a place where there is an iron ore bed, and there is a vast many men employed in digging the ore. The company that owns the ore bed have built quite a large town in about four years right in the wilds. There is a railroad to it. They take the ore away in the cars.

Your father and I and Eliza went out to see Ann last Thursday week. It was a fine day and we had a pleasant drive. I took her your children's photographs. She was quite delighted with them.

The weather here has been very wet and cold. We have not had one really warm day all the spring. I wish you could have seen our place when the trees were all out in bloom. I thought I never saw anything so pretty.

I received a letter from Helen last week. She writes to me about every three weeks, and little Alf encloses one in his Ma's. He will be eight years old next September I think. I don't know how long Joseph has to go to college but I think three or four years. We are expecting them up in August to make a visit. Ann is coming home then to see them, and Sarah talks of coming down this summer. How I wish you were coming, and if all was well what fine times we could have.

Alfred has just come in. He says I am to give his love to you. Your father joins with me in kindest love to you both and the dear children.

Your affectionate Father and Mother

PART THREE: AT HOME IN UPPER CANADA

Letter 22

Rawdon
June 25th, 1870

My dearest Daughter and Son,

I am afraid my dear girl you will think as usual that I have been long answering your kind and welcome letter. I see yours is dated February 16 and now it is almost the last of June. I would often think I would sit down and write to you and something would prevent me, and so the time passed by, but I hope you will forgive me. I hope to do better the next time.

The weather here is very hot and dry. Your father is going to begin mowing his clover and timothy grass tomorrow, but it is not nearly so good as it was last year. All crops were very abundant last year and we had a nice cool summer. The showers seemed to come just as we wanted them, but it is not so now. Everything is scorching up and it is so fearfully hot night and day, I feel almost troubled to stand it sometimes. I hope it will please God to send rain soon.

Just now my dear since I have been writing there has come up heavy thunder and we have had a beautiful shower of rain. It made my garden look so pretty. How I wish you could all pack up and make us a year's visit. Oh how happy we should be to see you once more on this earth. I was so pleased to hear you could remember us. Your father has not changed as much as you might think. He is much stouter than he used to be and looks very well for his years.

I was so pleased with the description you have of our old home. It seemed to bring everything back so fresh to my memory. If you were here I should never want to go to England. We have a very comfortable home here all our own. We have only fifty acres of land, and that is as much as your father wants to work now. Your father has worked very hard all the years he has been here, but he is not able to work so now, and I am thankful that he is not obliged to do so. The forty-five acres he bought from Joseph he sold again this spring for 500 dollars. He would not have sold it, but he was not able to go there to work it for if you send men away alone it doesn't pay. They want big wages and don't care to do much for them, some of them.

I must tell you now that Helen has got a little daughter born, I think, April 12th, and she calls her Sarah Sophia or Sophia Sarah, I don't know which. She is gone from Kingston this summer. Joseph was sent as missionary to the County of Lanark. When he got there the people had a house furnished ready for his family, so he wrote back to Helen to get ready and he came back after her. She wrote me word she took nothing with them, only their clothes and a few dishes.

A NEW LIFE IN CANADA

She says they are very comfortable. Joseph has visited over fifty families since he has been there, and they all received him in the kindest way. I am so glad Helen and the children could go with him for she would have been lonesome in Kingston for four or five months without him. It was so different when she was close to us.

I am expecting Sarah to visit us this summer. I hope she will come, but she has so much business, I am almost afraid she will not. Your father and I were out to see Ann last week. She was very busy. She has such a lot of work, she has two apprentices with her. She makes money fast. Eliza and Munroe are both well. Eliza sends her fondest love to you. Her two little children grow nicely. They are two sweet little children. Edgar and his wife are well, but some of his children have sore eyes and they can't get them cured. Edgar has been twice to Montreal this spring with fat cattle. Tell little Anne her Granma was so glad to hear she went to school, and give my fondest love to Alfred. I should be so pleased to get another letter from him.

We are likely to have a nice lot of apples and a good many cherries but not so many as we had last year. How are your hops? I have three hills at the bottom of the garden, and they look beautiful. Everything is forward here this summer, some say three weeks more than it was ever known. I have eight cows this summer. We churn every morning. It makes quite a lot of work, but I like to have them whilst I can look after them.

Please give my love to my sisters if you see them. Your father joins with me in kindest love to you and Christopher and both the children, and believe us to remain your affectionate parents,

Alfred and Sophia Eastwood

ACTIVITIES

Activities

Part One: The Journey

Letters 1 - 6

Pre-reading Discussion:

People emigrate for many different reasons. What are some of these reasons?

How might they choose their new country once they have decided to emigrate?

Many people have emigrated to Canada recently and in the past. What do you think influenced their decision?

Have you ever emigrated from one country to another, or do you know anyone who has? Discuss first impressions. Were there surprises? disappointments?

Responding to the Letters:

What did you find most interesting in these letters? Find a passage that you enjoyed and read it to the class. Explain why you chose it.

In small groups or with a partner answer the following questions:

1.   Why do you think the Eastwoods decided to emigrate?

2.   Compare their journey with that of a modern emigrant family.

3.   The Eastwoods had both pleasant and unpleasant experiences as passengers on board ship. Describe two or three of each of these. How did they respond?

4.   What would have made their ocean voyage more comfortable? more difficult?

5.   The Eastwoods have been in Upper Canada for a year at the conclusion of Letter 6. Was it an easy year? What problems have they had? How have they solved them?

6. From what you now know about the Eastwoods, do you think they will be successful in Canada? Give a reason for your answer.

7. Make a list of questions you would like to ask members of the Eastwood family about their experiences so far?

8. Have you ever been in a situation where your expectations were not met? Describe it and explain what you did about it.

Note-Taking:

Write in point form the main events in each letter. Note which information is a continuation from the previous letter and which is new.

Writing:

Complete one or more of the following activities:

(Exchange your work with a classmate for comments, and then be prepared to read it to a group or to the class before handing it in.)

1. Write a letter to a grandparent, Laura, or Thomas from Sarah's or Edgar's point of view describing either the journey from England or the first year in Upper Canada.

2. During their first year in Canada the Eastwoods decided to move into "the heart of the forest." What might have led them to make this decision? Using information from your notes write a composition explaining and justifying their actions.

3. Imagine you are an author developing a character for a story. Describe Sarah or Edgar in detail. Begin by gathering information from your notes; then add as much as you can from your imagination. Include a physical description, attitudes and reactions, usual and unusual behaviour, role in the family, hopes for the future. Include typical comments he or she might make.

ACTIVITIES

Language:

With a partner determine the meaning of each of the following phrases or sentences. Then write them in other words. Compare your answers with a classmate's.

1. We had gone a great many miles yesterday before I knew we were started (Letter 1).

2. We have had no seasickness worth speaking of yet (2).

3. "Tis a heaven for women but a bad place for men and horses" (4).

4. We are just as well off as I thought we should be (4).

5. So you may see we are not flowing with milk and honey some describe it to be (5).

6. I did not find it as I expected and I had not much heart for shooting (5).

7. It is not such a one as we shall build some day (6).

8. We could keep any quantity of stock if we could buy it (6).

Using a Table: The Eastwood Family Tree

With a partner study the Eastwood family tree and write answers to these questions:

1. How old were Sophia and Alfred Eastwood when they emigrated from England? How many children did they have? When was their youngest child born?

2. How old were Sarah and Edgar in 1843? Do you think they were old enough to be hired out as servants? What can you learn about Thomas from the family tree?

3. Laura, who was too ill to travel when the family left England, never saw her parents again. How old was she when they left? when her mother died?

4. Did all Sophia and Alfred's children reach adulthood? Who married? Who did not? According to the family tree, how many grandchildren did Sophia and Alfred have?

69

5.   Who lived longer, Sophia or Alfred? Did they outlive any of their children? If so who?

6.   In general, what can be learned from a family tree? What information would you like to see added to this one?

7.   Using the Eastwoods' family tree as a model, develop one for your own or another family.

Role-Play Suggestions:

In groups develop a short skit for one of the situations outlined below, or create one of your own based on the letters. Write out the script and then present your skit to the class.

1.   A mother and father are discussing emigration.

    a.   advantages/disadvantages
    b.   where to go
    c.   how each family member might benefit, help
    d.   making a decision

2.   The family is in a very crowded part of the ship.

    a.   recognize the problem
    b.   discuss alternatives
    c.   take action
    d.   assess the new situation

3.   Seeing Canada for the first time.

    a.   first reactions, for example to landscape and weather
    b.   plans for the first day
    c.   saying goodbye to new friends made on the journey
    d.   disembarking; immediate tasks and responsibilities

4.   Looking for work.

    a.   skills of individuals in family
    b.   work available and preferences
    c.   employment: asking, getting, accepting
    d.   terms, expectations, duration, payment

Part Two: Into the Wildwood

Letters 7 - 15

Responding to the Letters:

Skim through the letters you have just read. Find an activity or event described by Sophia that you found interesting or would like to try. Read the description to your class or group, and explain why you chose it.

Note-Taking: Continue to take notes as in Part One.

Writing:

1. Imagine that you are a modern journalist writing an article about an aspect of life in the bush.

Find in your notes as much information as you can about one of these topics:

    food
    health
    farming
    marriage
    a topic of your choice

Refer back to the letters if you wish. Organize your information and write an article about it. Include quotations from the letters to support your points. Consider adding an illustration or diagram.

Ask a classmate to read and comment on a draft of your article before you write it in final form.

2. Reread Edgar's note to Thomas at the end of Letter 10. Write the note from Thomas to which Edgar was replying.

A NEW LIFE IN CANADA

Language:

Imagine Edgar and Thomas took up school teaching or another line of work instead of farming. Write the notes they might have sent to each other.

2.   The Eastwoods never used the word "pioneer" to describe themselves or their experiences. Why do you think we do?

Are there phrases or words in the letters that are unfamiliar to you? Together with a partner identify some of them and determine their meanings.

List some current words and phrases that the Eastwoods might not understand.

Reading Pictures:

Study the drawing with Letter 6 (page 29) and photograph accompanying Letter 7(page 23), and with a classmate answer these questions:

1.   What stage in a settler's life do they show?

2.   How are they the same and different?

3.   Which do you find more interesting?

4.   Is one necessarily more accurate than the other? Explain why or why not.

5.   What are some advantages of photographs? some disadvantages?

6.   Can artists control their subject matter in ways that photographers cannot? Explain.

Role-Play Suggestions:

1.   Choosing land.

   a. needs and priorities of the family
   b. skills and abilities
   c. considering several properties
   d. making a decision

ACTIVITIES

2.   Visiting a new neighbour.

   a. greetings and introductions
   b. exchange of questions
   c. offers of help
   d. arranging future visits or a bee

3.   An offer of marriage.

   a. making and receiving the proposal
   b. family discussion
   c. accepting or rejecting
   d. future plans

4.   Explaining how to make or do something.

   a. reason for
   b. materials and equipment needed
   c. procedure
   d. putting it to use

5.   An illness or injury.

   a. cause; symptoms
   b. getting help, advice
   c. progress of disease or injury
   d. recovery

Part Three: At Home in Upper Canada

Letters 16 - 22

Responding to the Letters:

Sophia ended her correspondence with her daughter Laura on a positive note. What did she say in her last letter that suggested she was happy in Canada? Based on what you have read, would you say she and Alfred were successful? Why or why not?

In what ways was Part Three different from Parts One and Two? What did all three have in common? Which period in the Eastwoods' lives did you find most interesting? Explain why.

Tell the story of one person in the family. Why did you choose this person?

Study the photograph of Alfred and Sophia Eastwood. What can you learn about them from it? What does it leave out? Why was photography so important to Sophia?

Language:

Working with a partner find phrases or sentences in the letters that:

1. suggest life has become a little easier for the Eastwoods

2. indicate that the local community has grown and developed

3. make reference to events of interest or concern to the people of Upper Canada generally

Note-Taking:

Take notes for the letters in **Part Three**.

ACTIVITIES

Writing:

Review your notes. Then read over the list of topics suggested below. Using one of them write an essay, a narrative poem, a play, or a story.

Suggested Topics:

1. Sophia Eastwood: An ordinary woman, an extraordinary life.

2. A biography of Sarah or Edgar Eastwood.

3. A Family Portrait.

4. Into the Wildwood.

5. The importance to the Eastwoods of their first year in Upper Canada.

6. "Tis a heaven for women but a bad place for men and horses." Consider this statement as it relates to the experience of the Eastwood family.

7. A topic of your choice.

Working with Graphics:

Between 1844 and 1870 the Eastwoods changed the appearance and use of their land. Draw a diagram or plan of their farm as it might have looked in 1870. Consider using color, a legend, or labels.

Role-Play Outlines:

1. A Cash Crop.

    a. good harvest; deciding to sell
    b. the marketplace; negotiating
    c. a buyer; agreeing
    d. reviewing the day's events

A NEW LIFE IN CANADA

2. Holiday Gathering.

    a. arrivals, family and friends
    b. exchange of news
    c. present giving, receiving
    d. at dinner

3. Shopping for something new.

    a. what is needed and why
    b. where and when to go
    c. choosing carefully; paying
    d. showing, sharing, using new purchase

4. The second house.

    a. compare with first dwelling
    b. materials, construction, size
    c. inside and outside
    d. the surrounding area

5. The early years and the later years compared.

    a. way of life
    b. work
    c. comforts
    d. the family

ACTIVITIES

Concluding Activities:

1. Imagine it is sometime between 1840 and 1870, and you are the editor of a local newspaper. Design and produce the front page for an issue of your paper.

2. With a partner or small group complete the activity below:

Choosing a Farm

Imagine you are going to buy a farm. Make a list of the features you would most like it to have. Arrange these in order of importance.

Now read the descriptions below. Which farm will you choose? Reach agreement within your group, and be prepared to explain your decision to the class.

What will you do first when you move to your new farm?

I	II	III
•good soil •small (40 acres) •expensive per acre •good financing •price includes equipment and livestock •other work near •water (well) •neighbours •no school nearby •buildings: small house, barn •no pasture: 10 acres mixed hardwood bush •flat land	•large (100 acres) •inexpensive but cash down required •good crop land •water (stream) •unpaved road to property •never farmed •good financing •no buildings nearby •few neighbours •good pasture and hardwood forest •good view	•large (100 acres) •on a lake •rocky soil •near town •school near •medium price/ low down payment •work available •neighbours •barn and shed only; no house •pine woods and pasture

77

A NEW LIFE IN CANADA

Extensions:

1. Arrange a visit to Toronto's First Post Office. It is located at 260 Adelaide Street East, Toronto, M5A 1N1. A variety of educational, special, and interpretive programs are offered.

2. Visit a pioneer village, museum, or site such as Black Creek Pioneer Village, Upper Canada Village, or the Canadiana Gallery in Toronto.

3. Try to visit a modern working farm. If you live or have worked on a farm, compare your experience with the Eastwoods'.

4. Develop a timeline for Canada from 1800 to 1900. Create a parallel timeline for the Eastwood family.

5. Videotape or photograph class dramatizations of the Eastwoods' experiences. Consider making a tape of farm sounds to accompany your work. Share a live or video production with another group or class.

6. Arrange to try one or more pioneer arts or crafts.

Suggestions for Independent Learning:

1. Canada was inhabited for many years before the arrival of Europeans. Use your library resource centre to find out about Canada's original people. You might wish to concentrate on the life and culture of a specific group, or you might prefer to study an element such as legend or myth.

2. The French were the first Europeans to settle permanently in Canada. Read about the role of France in Canadian history and about the settlement of Quebec by the French.

3. Learn about immigration to Canada in the nineteenth century from several points of view.

4. A number of Canadian women wrote about their experiences during this period. Susanna Moodie, Catharine Parr Traill, and Anna Jameson are three of these. Read some of their work, and explore the literature of nineteenth century Canada generally.

5. Find out about life in the towns and cities of Upper Canada during the nineteenth century.

6. Read about education in Ontario before 1900, the programs offered and the expectations of the pupils and their families. If possible, read some early textbooks.

7. Study the pioneer stage in Upper Canada's development and determine to what extent the Eastwoods' experience was typical. Learn about your own area.

8. Read about Confederation and how and why it was achieved.

9. Compare recent immigration procedures and experiences with these in the nineteenth century from the point of view of the government or an immigrant.

Glossary

Letter 1

steamer tugged to the vessel: the sailing ship was guided down the Thames by a steamboat.

steerage: a section in a passenger ship for those paying the lowest fares.

Letter 2

Dover: port city in south-east England; the part of England closest to France; famous for its white cliffs.

Letter 3

put into the Mighty Deep: buried at sea.

fishing smack: a fishing boat with two sails and a well in which fish are kept alive.

sea hogs: porpoises.

Frant: a village in Sussex, England; home of Alfred Eastwood's mother.

A NEW LIFE IN CANADA

Letter 4

The Plains of Abraham: overlooks the St. Lawrence River; scene of battle September 13, 1759 between the French and the British. As a result of this battle, Quebec was secured for the British. Both leaders, the Marquis de Montcalm and General James Wolfe, were killed.

batteries: places where artillery is mounted.

hired a room: rented a room.

took shipping: bought a ticket.

stopped: stayed.

pounds, shillings, pence: British currency, widely used in Upper Canada.

Bytown: renamed Ottawa in 1855.

dear: expensive.

gig: a light, two-wheeled carriage.

hops: plants used in making beer.

Letter 5

sovereign: a British coin; gold; worth one pound.

Miskins: the Sussex home of Sophia Eastwood's parents.

English Church: Church of England.

game: a wild animal or bird that is hunted.

dray: a low, flat cart, used for heavy loads.

GLOSSARY

Letter 6

potash: obtained from wood ash; used for making soap; the first source of cash for many pioneers.

vitals: victuals; food.

Letter 7

underbrushed: cleared away forest undergrowth in preparation for chopping down the trees.

Letter 8

rheumatics: having to do with rheumatism; may cause an inflammation of the muscles and joints.

to be out: work as a servant for a family.

Aldeny cow: Alderney, a breed of cattle.

Letter 9

it all came good: it all grew.

timothy grass: a coarse grass used for animal feed.

get their living: find enough to eat.

yoke of cattle: two animals that work together.

grist mill: a mill where farmers could have their grain ground.

carding mill: a mill where fibers are prepared for weaving.

Letter 10

ague: a malarial type attack of chills and fever.

bespeak: arrange for.

A NEW LIFE IN CANADA

Letter 13

all our dependence: our only source of income.

innards: internal organs; an animal's insides.

rosin: a substance made from turpentine.

Letter 16

meeting: church service.

granary: building for storing grain.

Letter 17

hewed: shaped with an axe.

sash windows: windows that open by sliding up and down.

Letter 19

The War in the States: the war between the North and the South in the United States: 1861-1865.

Yellow Fever: a serious infection caused by mosquitoes.

Letter 20

Fenians: members of an Irish nationalist organization that wanted to overthrow British rule. They were first organized in New York in 1857 but gained notoriety for staging a series of raids into Canada in the 1860's.

METRIC CONVERSIONS

1 pound (16 ounces) = 454 grams or 0.454 kilogram

1 ton (2000 pounds) = 0.907 tonnes

1 inch = 2.54 centimetres

1 foot (12 inches) = 30.48 centimetres

1 yard (3 feet; 36 inches) = 0.9144 metre

1 mile (5280 feet) = 1.6 kilometres

1 acre (4840 sq. yd.) = .405 hectares

1 bushel (4 pecks; 8 gallons) = .36.4 litres

1 gallon (4 quarts; 8 pints) = 4.546 litres British Imperial

PHOTO CREDITS

Cover	Alfred and Sophia Eastwood	Metropolitan Toronto Library (MTL)
Letter 1	At the agent's office	Public Archives of Canada (PAC)
Letter 2	Forecastle at midday	Royal Ontario Museum (ROM)
Letter 4	Montreal	PAC
Letter 4	Steamboat Ad	PAC
Letter 5	Picton	MTL
Letter 5	Walk in woods	PAC
Letter 6	Quilting Bee	Art Gallery of Ontario (AGO)
Letter 6	Entering the Woods	PAC
Letter 7	Cabin interior	Ontario Archives (OA)
Letter 7	Cabin exterior	OA
Letter 8	Sleighing	ROM
Letter 9	Plowing	OA
Letter 10	Carrying a deer	OA
Letter 11	Bush clearing	PAC
Letter 12	Ox cart and family	OA
Letter 13	Schoolhouse	OA
Letter 14	House building bee	OA
Letter 15	Bush clearing	PAC
Letter 17	Men squaring logs	OA
Letter 18	New house interior	OA
Letter 18	Growing Village	OA
Letter 19	Children with cart	ROM
Letter 21	Lang's farm	ROM